ARCHERY
FOR FUN!

By Jana Voelke Studelska

Content Adviser: Lloyd Brown, National Archery Association, Level 5 Master Coach, San Diego, California
Reading Adviser: Frances J. Bonacci, Ed.D., Reading Specialist, Cambridge, Massachusetts

Compass Point Books ✦ Minneapolis, Minnesota

Compass Point Books
3109 West 50th Street, #115
Minneapolis, MN 55410

Photographs ©: Lawrence Sawyer/iStockphoto, cover (top left); Cloki/Shutterstock, cover (bottom left); Sean Gladwell/Shutterstock, cover (middle), back cover; Robert J. Beyers II/Shutterstock, cover (right), 19 (right), 38–39, 47; David Crowther/iStockphoto, 4–5; Kenneth V. Pilon/Shutterstock, 6; The Print Collector/Photolibrary, 7; The Granger Collection, New York, 9 (left), 42 (all); North Wind Picture Archives, 9 (right); Karon Dubke/Capstone Press, 10, 11 (left), 26, 27, 30, 31 (all); Jessica Bilén/BigStockPhoto, 11 (right), 17 (bottom); Kim Steele/Photographer's Choice/Getty Images, 12; Greg Ceo/Riser/Getty Images, 13 (top); Christine Balderas/iStockphoto, 13 (bottom); N Joy Neish/Shutterstock, 15; Pratt-Pries/Photononstop/Art Life Images, 16 (top); Jeff Griffin/iStockphoto, 16 (bottom); Dave King/Dorling Kindersley/Getty Images, 17 (top & middle); Alex Segre/Alamy, 18–19; Ryan Lindberg/Shutterstock, 20; Bojan Tezak/iStockphoto, 21; Comstock Images/Jupiter Images, 23; Rhouck/Dreamstime, 24; Andrew Barker/Shutterstock, 25; Image100/Jupiter Images, 28–29; Peter-John Freeman/iStockphoto, 29 (bottom); Franc Podgoršek/Shutterstock, 32–33; Shariff Che'Lah/Dreamstime, 33 (bottom); Private Collection/Look and Learn/The Bridgeman Art Library, 34; Harry Shepherd/Fox Photos/Getty Images, 35; Romeo Gacad/AFP/Getty Images, 36–37; AP Images/Ben Curtis, 37 (front); AP Images/Hays Daily News, Jamie Roper, 39 (right); AP Images/Katsumi Kasahara, 40; Cathrin Mueller/Bongarts/Getty Images, 41; Dynamic Graphics/Jupiter Images, 43 (left); AP Images/Dominique Mollard, 43 (right); John Kobal Foundation/Getty Images, 44 (left); Private Collection/The Stapleton Collection/The Bridgeman Art Library, 44 (right); AP Images, 45.

Editor: Brenda Haugen
Page Production: Ashlee Schultz
Photo Researcher: Eric Gohl
Creative Director: Keith Griffin
Editorial Director: Nick Healy
Managing Editor: Catherine Neitge

Library of Congress Cataloging-in-Publication Data
Studelska, Jana Voelke.
  Archery for fun! / by Jana Voelke Studelska.
     p. cm. — (For fun)
  Includes index.
  ISBN 978-0-7565-3390-8 (library binding)   1. Archery—Juvenile literature.
  2. Archery—History—Juvenile literature. I. Title. II. Series.
  GV1189.S88 2008
  799.3'2—dc22   2007032686

Visit Compass Point Books on the Internet at www.compasspointbooks.com
or e-mail your request to custserv@compasspointbooks.com

Table of Contents

The Basics

Doing It

People, Places, and Fun

Note: In this book, there are two kinds of vocabulary words. Archery Words to Know are words specific to archery. They are defined on page 46. Other Words to Know are helpful words that aren't related only to archery. They are defined on page 47.

The Beginning of Archery

It would be hard to think of a sport older than archery. The oldest cave drawings show archers hunting animals, and scientists have found 50,000-year-old arrow points in Africa.

Think of it. Civilization was created as people began to make food, clothes, and shelter from animals that archers had shot. Tribes, nations, and empires protected themselves with bows and arrows. Soldiers and warriors shot arrows from horseback, chariots, castles, and ships. As time went on, new designs came along that allowed arrows to pierce a knight's armor or travel long distances.

While there are still remote tribes that rely on archery to survive, most of today's archers simply enjoy the challenge of trying to shoot an arrow right into their target. Some are hunters, some are competitive or Olympic athletes, and some, like you, are people who enjoy the tradition and have the skill required to handle a bow and arrow.

How Does a Bow Work?

A bow can be thought of as a pair of springs connected in the middle by the handle and kept in tension by a string. When the string is pulled back, energy is created. When the string is released, the energy is released and transferred to the arrow. That energy is powerful! If you release a string without an arrow to shoot, your bow can crack and break.

Archery Makes History

The earliest archers used bone, sinew, wood, stone, and other materials to create the first bows and arrows. Places where craftspeople made arrowheads have been found.

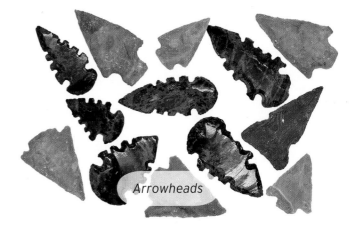
Arrowheads

The ancient Egyptians' bows were as tall as humans. These bows had arrowheads made of flint or bronze at the tip. The king's arrows were made with gold!

People known as Assyrians created a shorter bow with a new shape called a recurve. It was powerful and small enough that archers could shoot from horseback, allowing the Assyrians to defeat the Egyptians.

Soldiers continued to improve the design of their bows and arrows,

6

giving them superior battle power. The Romans, the Parthians, and the Mongols are just some of the mighty archers who made history by defeating one another and dominating the civilizations of Europe and Asia.

The availability of gunpowder and firearms in the 1600s changed the ways of war.

No longer were bows and arrows used on the battlefield. Archery became a sport, often practiced by rich and powerful noblemen and royalty.

Concentrate!

From 1327 to 1377, the English royalty banned all sports other than archery. The king believed that his subjects should practice archery, not waste time on other sports. Practiced archers were important to defending England from invaders. A royal decree in 1363 required all Englishmen to practice archery on Sundays and holidays.

Native American Archery

In North America, Native Americans developed bows and arrows different from those invented across the oceans. Though their bows may have been simple, Native Americans used them with skill. In fact, Native Americans fought, and often won, battles with European invaders armed with guns.

Some Native American bows were made for use on foot. They were larger than those made for use on horseback. The Dakota made bowstrings from the necks of snapping turtles. Inuit made arrows from wood and ptarmigan feathers.

The Native American bows and arrows were more than just weapons. They were also used in religious ceremonies as symbols of magic and power.

A Little-Known Fact

Until the 1870s, Native Americans may have been the only archers in North America. After the Civil War, brothers Will and Maurice Thompson moved into the wilderness to learn archery from Native Americans in Florida. The brothers wrote a book about their experience called *The Witchery of Archery*. The book became quite popular, and the sport of archery gained national attention. When the first national archery tournament was held in 1879, Will Thompson won. He was champion five more times.

Basic Tackle and Targets

Archery equipment is called tackle. The basics are the bow and the arrow. And you'll need a target, of course!

Professional and experienced archers use fancy, expensive equipment, but you can get started with just a few simple things.

arrowhead with target point

nock

fletching

shaft

index feather

crest

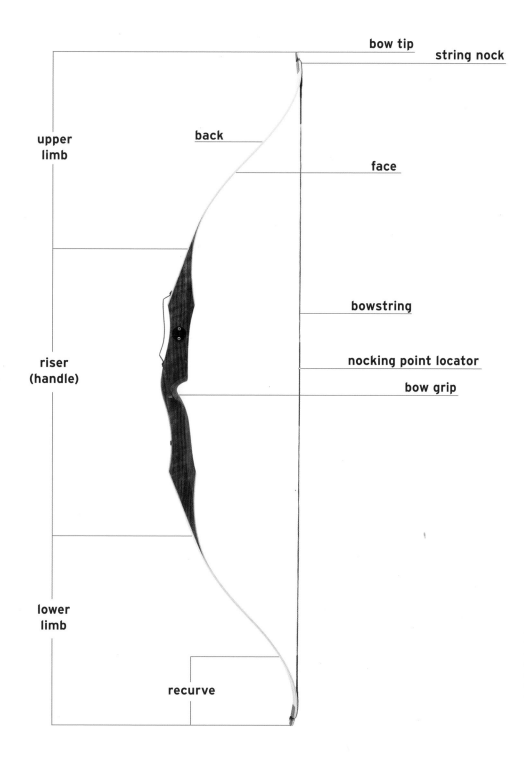

bow tip
string nock
upper limb
back
face
riser (handle)
bowstring
nocking point locator
bow grip
lower limb
recurve

Scoring Zones

Each color on a target has two equal scoring areas, divided by a line. If you hit the center of the gold zone, you score 10. If you hit the outer edge of the gold zone, you get a score of nine. The numbers get smaller as you go farther from the gold center to the white outer ring.

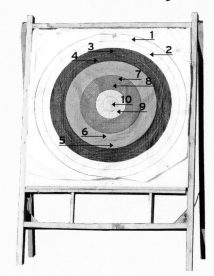

Types of Bows

Each type of bow is designed for a specific job or competition. And each bow will shoot differently, even if it's made by the same manufacturer or bowyer, a person who makes bows by hand. Try as many bows as you can.

Long bow

Long bow: A long bow is a traditional bow. The design is simple. However, a long bow doesn't have great speed.

Recurve bow: A recurve bow has tips that curve forward, away from the archer. When the bowstring is pulled, the tips straighten. This design provides plenty of spring, allowing the arrow to be released with much more energy. A recurve bow is a good, less-expensive bow for a beginner learning the basics.

Compound bow: A compound bow has a system of pulleys and cables that allows an archer to hold a full draw without much effort. Most hunters use compound bows.

Compound bow

Crossbow: A crossbow is mounted sideways onto a gun stock, or the butt of the gun. The string is pulled back by the archer but is held in place by the trigger. Crossbows have a long history as lethal weapons of warfare and hunting. A crossbow shooter is referred to as a crossbowman, not an archer.

Crossbow

Flight bow: Flight bows are short, stiff, and powerful. They're used for distance shooting and are difficult to master.

Take-down bow: A take-down bow is made of pieces that can be taken apart, making it easier to store and transport. This bow also allows an archer to replace or upgrade one piece at a time. Competitive archers often use take-down bows. There are many inexpensive take-down bows available. They are a great choice for beginners.

Composite bow: Composite bows are made with two or more materials, such as wood, fiberglass, or aluminum. The use of multiple materials gives bows more strength, flexibility, and power.

Varieties of Arrows

When choosing arrows, there are many things to consider. You'll need to match the stiffness of the arrow to the weight of the bow using your draw length (see pages 22-23). You'll want to think about the thickness of the shaft, the length and weight of the arrow, and the material the arrow is made from.

Go to an archery shop where a trained salesperson can show you the proper arrows for a beginner. Some stores even

Fletching and Vanes

Feathers on the ends of arrows are called fletching. Arrows with fletching are often used for indoor shooting. Outdoors, weather may affect the fletching, so archers usually use arrows with other materials on the ends, such as plastic. Any materials other than feathers on the ends of arrows are called vanes. Fletching and vanes affect the flight of arrows. A flu-flu arrow, for example, has extra fletching for more wind resistance, which keeps it from traveling far.

Fiberglass arrows don't cost much either, but they're more durable than wood. However, fiberglass arrows are heavy and have a harder time going longer distances.

Aluminum arrows are a good all-around choice. They can get wet or hit rocks and suffer little breakage or bending. Aluminum arrows come in many sizes. These arrows are often used by hunters.

have target areas for testing your choices before you buy.

Wood arrows are the least expensive, least accurate, and least durable. If you're a beginner, your accuracy is probably not great anyway, so using wood might be a good idea until you gain some skill.

Carbon arrows are lightweight, smaller in diameter than aluminum, and very stiff. Carbon arrows are easy to use and can be a good choice for beginners.

Aluminum-carbon arrows are used by advanced archers. These are the arrows used to set world records.

The Finishing Touch

You don't need anything but a bow, an arrow, and a target to begin archery. But some people feel that a few extra items can help them improve their shot.

Arm guards protect your arm from getting whacked by the bowstring when it's released. Make sure yours is snug.

Scopes help you aim at your target and see where your arrows are hitting. Some scopes are mounted on bows, and others are handheld.

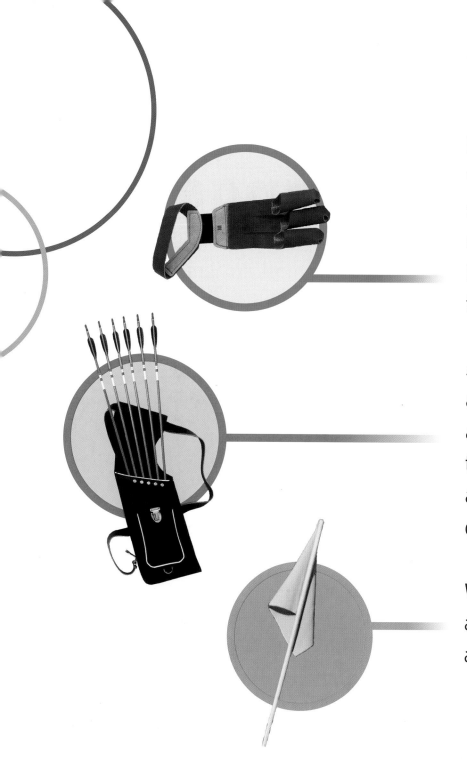

Finger tabs are worn over the fingers of your shooting hand. They can give you a smooth release. A three-fingered shooting glove does the same job as finger tabs, but it has more coverage. You can try both to decide which you like better.

Arrows are kept in a **quiver**. Not many archers wear the quiver on their backs anymore. Most have a belt quiver, making the arrows easy to reach. Others prefer a ground quiver, which sticks into the ground next to you.

Wind flags help you judge wind direction and strength. You can make your own with a piece of cloth.

Rules of the Range

Archery has a great safety record because most archers follow the basic rules on the archery range. In fact, you're more likely to suffer bug bites and sunburn than be hurt by an arrow!

Archers sometimes injure wrists, hands, fingers, or inner arms. These are the muscles that work the hardest. Always see a doctor if you are unsure of how hurt you might be.

On the archery range, the range captain is in charge of all shooters. Follow the range captain's commands, and keep these rules in mind:

- Check all your equipment for cracks and twisting before shooting.

- Shoot only at a target that will stop an arrow. Make sure the target is placed in a safe direction.

- Wait for the range captain's command before starting to shoot.

- After you're done shooting, wait for the word "Clear!" from the range captain. Then you know it is safe to retrieve your arrows.

Strength, Endurance, and Flexibility

To be an archer, your muscles need to be toned and strong. Most of the muscles you use in archery will be in your upper body, such as your hands, arms, shoulders, and stomach.

The following exercises can be done at home. If you can use a gym, ask a trainer to help you develop a program for your archery workout.

Eagle wings: With weights (or cans of soup) in each hand, sit on a chair and raise your arms out straight, like wings. Hold for five seconds, then lower your arms and rest. Repeat 10 times.

Holding the draw: To strengthen your shooting muscles, draw the bow, and hold it for six seconds. Then relax, and slowly return the bowstring to the resting position. By changing the arm you use to draw the bow, you can work both sides of your body. It will feel awkward, but it's important to keep your body strong on both sides.

Sit-ups: Lie flat on your back. With your hands on your upper chest, raise your shoulders and head so they just come off the floor. Swing each elbow, one at a time, toward the opposite knee. Rest, and repeat.

Arm pulls: Sling your arm over your opposite shoulder, and hold it in place with your free hand behind the elbow. Turn your head to look away from your arms, and hold for 10 seconds. Switch to stretch the other side.

Body twists: Stand straight with your back a few inches away from a wall. Keeping your feet and knees facing forward as much as you're able, twist your upper body back to the wall, and try to place your hands on the wall. Switch to the other side.

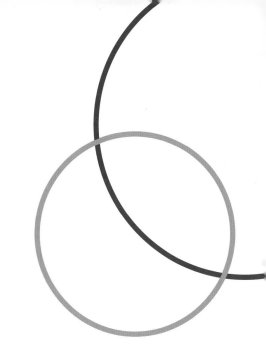

Measuring Up

Your tackle must be sized for your body and strength. You need to know your draw length, bow size, and arrow size, and which eye is dominant.

To find your draw length, you'll use a light bow and long arrow and pull with the arm that you would normally use to shoot. By measuring the arrow as it's pulled back into full draw, you find your draw length. It's best to have an experienced archer help you.

Your draw length determines the best size and type of bow for you to choose. The arrow size also depends on your draw length. You need arrows long enough to stay on the arrow rest at full draw, but they should not be too long.

The draw weight is the number of pounds or kilograms of force required to pull the bow a given distance. This number is printed on the bow, near the handle grip. If your draw length is shorter than the

standard for the bow you're using, it means you'll be shooting with less power.

Lastly, your eyes are not the same. It's important to identify which is your dominant eye. A shooter should have the bowstring directly in front of the dominant eye.

Which Eye Is Your Dominant Eye?

Hold your arms out in front of you, and make a small triangle with your thumbs and forefingers. With both eyes open, look at something in the distance, such as a doorknob, through the opening you've created with your hands. Close your left eye. If the object is still in your triangle view, you're right-eye dominant.

Now open just your left eye. The target object will appear to have moved out of your triangle view.

If you are right-eye dominant, you're probably right-handed and should shoot with a right-handed bow. If you are left-eye dominant, you're probably left-handed and should shoot with a left-handed bow.

What to Wear

Sometimes there are rules about what's allowed at competitive archery events. Many archers wear emblems of their clubs or logos of sponsoring companies. The group hosting the event may have rules about the colors of shirts and pants that are allowed.

If you're shooting for fun, you don't need anything special. Just make sure your clothes are tight-fitting to avoid contact with the string.

Good, sturdy shoes, such as tennis shoes, will help. Your stance is the foundation of your shooting.

If you have long hair, make sure it is pulled back so it doesn't get caught in your equipment.

White clothing will keep you cooler. It also makes you easy to see.

Some people find that their glasses interfere with their archery and choose to wear contact lenses. Others make sure they're wearing glasses designed for sports.

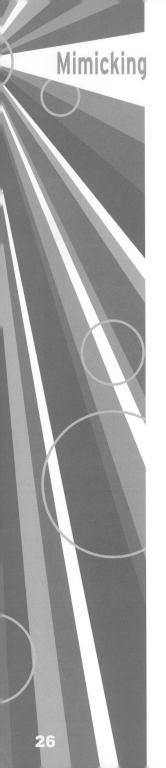

Practice Without Shooting

It's best to learn archery without an arrow. Mimicking—pretending to shoot, but without an arrow—will help you get used to the motions of shooting. Remember, never release the string from a full draw unless you have an arrow in place. Dry firing, which is firing without an arrow, may damage the bow.

Step 1: Stand sideways with your toes up against an imaginary line that points straight to the target.

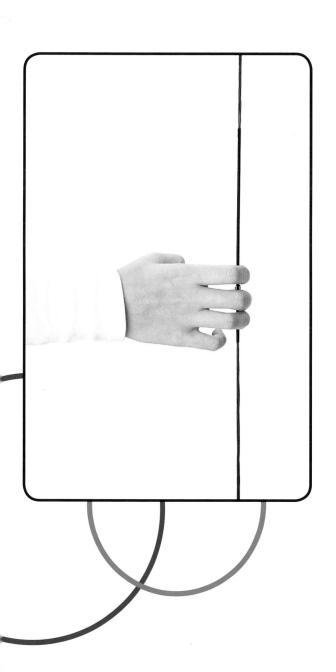

Step 2: Hold the bow at the grip, straight out in front of you.

Step 3: Use your middle three fingers to grip the bowstring, tucking the string into the crease of your first knuckle joints. Keep your wrist relaxed.

Step 4: Raise the bow until your bow arm is straight out from your shoulder. Rotate your bow arm until your elbow is facing down as much as possible.

Step 5: Draw the string back to anchor position, meaning where your draw hand stops, which is probably under your chin.

Step 6: Concentrate on the target, and notice your body's position and muscle tension.

Step 7: Slowly ease the string back to a resting position so you don't damage the bow.

Whoosh!

Now you're ready to shoot arrows. Be sure to follow safety rules.

Step 1: Stand in the shooting position you just learned.

Step 2: Snap the nock onto the string under the nock locator, making sure that the index feather sticks out toward your face.

Step 3: Place your hand on the bowstring with your index finger above the arrow and two fingers below the arrow.

Step 4: Raise the bow, and draw back to your anchor position. Assume T-form position.

Step 5: Concentrate on the target, and relax your string fingers. The string will release as you continue to hold your position.

What is T-form?

T-form is the shape of an archer's body at full draw. Your legs, torso, and head form a straight vertical line, and your arms a straight horizontal line, topping off the T.

Partner Up

Get an archery partner to look at you from the sides when you draw and shoot. Your partner will be able to give you feedback on your stance and shooting technique.

Practice Makes Perfect

The ability to shoot accurately depends on your ability to concentrate, as well as your strength. Holding a bow at anchor position takes muscles. Doing it six times in a row requires strength. Try these drills to improve your shooting.

Balloon Drill: Attach six inflated balloons on the target butt, the backing of a target. From a distance of 10 yards (9 meters), try popping the balloons. How many arrows does it take? Repeat, and enjoy your improving skills.

Paper Plate Drill: Pin a paper plate to a target backstop. From 10 yards (9 m) away, shoot an arrow at the plate. Pay careful attention to your T-form and stance. Now shoot six more arrows with your form as identical as possible to what you did in the first shot. Notice that it is more difficult to maintain your form as you shoot. Are your muscles tired? Retrieve your arrows, and repeat.

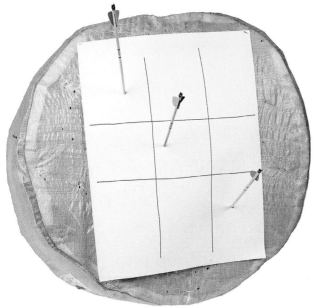

Tic-Tac-Toe: Draw a tic-tac-toe pattern on a big piece of paper. Mount it on the target butt, and begin playing. You can play by yourself or invite a fellow archer to join you.

Getting in the Game

Field archery

If you're lucky enough to live near an archery range or have a local archery club to join, you're on your way! Here are just some of the kinds of archery competitions you might want to check out.

Field archery started when bow hunters were looking for a natural setting in which to practice and compete. Archers shoot at targets of varying distances, often in rough terrain.

Most people start with target archery, because it's a great way to learn the basics. All types of bows can be used. Archers younger than 18 are divided into several age groups.

How about archery golf? Instead of 18 holes, there are 18 targets! Archers "tee off" with shots down the fairway, and try to complete the course with the fewest arrows.

Flight archery is all about distance. Archers need a good sense of aerodynamics to plan their shots. There are three classes of competition: target bows, flight bows, and freestyle. Freestyle archers don't stand and shoot. Instead, to gain more power for longer shots, they lie on their backs and pull back against the bows as they are held with their feet.

Crossbow shooting is a great spectator sport. The archers and equipment are interesting to watch, and the gatherings are usually as much celebration as they are competition.

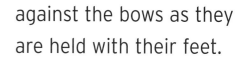

Target archery

The Legend of Robin Hood

Robin Hood was a legendary outlaw who lived in the 12th century. The first stories about him appeared in the 15th century.

Robin Hood was known for robbing from the rich to give to the poor. Ballads were written about many archers, but the stories of Robin Hood are the best known. With great

skill in archery, swordplay, and disguise, Robin Hood became a legend.

At least one part of the Robin Hood tales was true: archery tournaments. For hundreds of years English villages hosted tournaments. The tournaments lasted for days. People came from far and wide to feast, visit, and cheer the archery contestants. Archers would compete by shooting at balls thrown in the air, by shooting for distance, and by shooting arrows through armor.

Gold Medal Fever

Legend has it that the ancient Olympics began when Hercules, a Greek god and archer, held the games to honor his father, Zeus. The games were to have featured archers shooting at targets made of tethered doves. Yet there is no record of archery in the ancient Olympics, held from 776 B.C. to 393 A.D.

In fact, it wasn't until 1900 that archery showed up in the modern Olympics, and it didn't go well. International rules hadn't been developed, and each time the Games were held, the host country used its own rules. It was confusing for the archers. It also was hard to get a grandstand full of people to watch the competition. Soon, the Olympic Committee gave up on archery altogether.

Olympic Firsts
In 1904, the Olympics were held in the United States for the first time. St. Louis hosted the Games. Team archery was introduced, as was women's archery. American archers took first place in every archery contest, but they didn't have much competition. No other archers showed up!

In 1972, archery returned to the Olympics. An international set of rules for competition had been accepted by most countries. By the 1984 Los Angeles Games, the stands were packed with spectators. In 1992, Antonio Rebollo of the Spanish archery team shot a flaming arrow to ignite the Olympic torch at the opening ceremony.

Moving Up!

If you're into archery, the Junior Olympic Archery Development Program (JOAD) is your ticket to learning the sport. The organization is open to any girl or boy from ages 8 to 18.

JOAD was set up in 1967 to help train young archers. It sponsors clubs, contests, and classes and even helps train young athletes who hope to compete in the Olympics.

A club can be started when an adult leader with three or more young archers makes an application. You'll get information and instructions on shooting, as well as invitations to archery events. Archers receive pins to show their skill and ranking.

College Archery

Some colleges have official archery teams and offer scholarships to students with archery skills. Many of those students become members of the U.S. Archery Team, which trains archers for national and international competition.

Yabusame and Kyudo

Japan has a long history of archery. Many ceremonies and contests are still held. These celebrated events are attended by thousands of people.

Until the Middle Ages, shooting arrows while riding a horse running at full speed was a vital skill for Japanese warriors. Yabusame began as a form of military training combining horsemanship and archery.

Today archers wearing the hunting outfit of medieval warriors shoot at targets as they race by on horseback. The biggest event takes place every year on September 16 at

Tsurugaoka Hachiman Shrine in Kamakura. The event is more than a contest. It's a ceremony in which everyone prays for peace across the land. The contest arrows and targets are treasured as good-luck charms.

Kyudo means "the way of the bow." It is a tradition that comes from a time when warriors competed in archery

German archers practicing kyudo.

to see who had the greatest mental and physical strengths. Archers would try to shoot arrows through a long, narrow hall a few feet wide and tall, and more than 300 feet (91.4 m) long, without hitting the walls, floor, or ceiling. Each contestant would spend an entire day and night shooting arrows from a sitting position.

Many Japanese schools and universities teach archery. A national tournament takes place every year on Seijinnotti or coming-of-age day in January. Each archer aims several arrows at a target 66 yards (60 m) away. More than 1,000 people participate in the contest each year.

What Happened When?

50,000 B.C. **5000** **3000** **2000** **1000** **500 A.D.**

50,000 B.C.
The first stone
arrowheads are
created in Africa.

5000 B.C.
Egyptians begin
using the bow for
hunting and warfare.

2800 B.C.
Egyptians make the
first composite bows.

1500 B.C.
Chinese archery
is mentioned in
ancient texts.

1200 B.C. Soldiers
in chariots defeat
their enemies with an
advanced bow design.

500 A.D. Bows
and arrows are used
in North America.

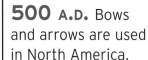

| 1400 | 1900 | 1960 | 1970 | 1980 | 1990 | 2000 |

1967 The Junior Olympic Archery Development Program is founded.

1363 The English king orders that archery be practiced every Sunday and on holidays

2007 The International Olympic Committee and Uganda Archery Foundation launched a campaign to promote archery in the eastern African country of Uganda.

1992 A flaming arrow ignites the Olympic torch at the the Barcelona Games.

1900 Archery competition is held at the modern Olympics for the first time.

2001 Many people are inspired to try archery after seeing Legolas in *The Lord of the Rings*.

Fun Archery Facts

The legend of Robin Hood may be true! In 2003, a secret escape tunnel was found under Nottingham Church in England. A medieval document tells a story in which Robin and his Merry Men are at the church, which was surrounded by the sheriff's soldiers. When the soldiers broke down the doors, Robin and the men were nowhere to be found.

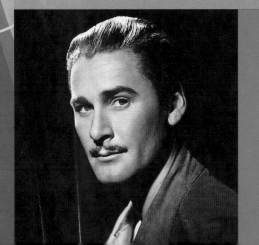

Errol Flynn, the actor who played the first Robin Hood on film, was coached by Howard Hill, a famous bow hunter. Warner Brothers Pictures wanted Flynn to become a convincing archer.

In 1991, in the melting edge of a glacier, a mountain climber in the Alps found the preserved body of a man who died about 5,000 years ago. The frozen hunter was dressed in leather clothes and a waterproof grass cloak. His shoes were stuffed with grass, for insulation. He had a framed backpack, a utility belt containing tools, and a quiver containing 14 arrows.

In Europe in 1252, each man owning land worth between 40 and 100 shillings was required to equip himself with a sword, dagger, bow, and arrows. Those owning land worth less than 40 shillings had to equip themselves with only bows and arrows.

In 1457, the king of England decreed that the sports of football (soccer) and golf would be banned because they interfered with archery practice.

45

Archery Words to Know

anchor position: place where the hand is held against the chin when at full draw

arm guard: stiff pad worn over the forearm to protect it from a snapping bowstring

composite bow: bow constructed of two or more materials, such as wood and fiberglass

compound bows: bows with cables and pulleys

crossbow: bow that is mounted on a gun stock

draw length: the measure of an arrow as it's pulled back into full draw

draw weight: weight required to pull a bowstring back a specific distance

dry firing: snapping the bowstring without an arrow in place

fletching: feathers on the end of an arrow

flight bow: bow specially made for flight shooting, in which the winner shoots an arrow the longest distance

index feather: feather in fletching that is a different color, marked to indicate the proper placement of the arrow

long bow: simple, traditional bow in the shape of an arc with no additional equipment attached

nock: slit in the arrow's end that is placed against the bowstring

nocking point locator: the spot on the string that marks where the arrow's nock should be placed

quiver: storage bag, or basket, for carrying arrows

recurve bow: bow design in which the tips of the bow bend away from the archer

scopes: tubes with telescopic lenses used to let archers better aim at their targets; some scopes are mounted on the bow, while others can be handheld

tackle: archery equipment

take-down bow: bow whose parts can be broken down for easy storage and travel

vanes: materials other than feathers placed on the ends of arrows

Other Words to Know

aerodynamics: study of the interaction between air and the solid bodies moving through it

Assyrians: group of people living on the Arabian peninsula around 700 B.C.

bronze: metal alloy made of copper and tin

emblems: embroidered symbols that represent a group of people

Mongols: nomadic people whose empire extended across Asia around 1200

Parthians: Greek-speaking people famous for their horse-mounted soldiers who fought against the Romans

ptarmigan: small chickenlike bird with feathered feet

sinew: animal tendon

tension: balanced tightness

tethered: tied together

Where to Learn More

MORE BOOKS TO READ

Boga, Steve. *Archery*. Mechanicsburg, Pa.: Stackpole Books, 1997.

Gurstelle, William. *The Art of the Catapult: Build Greek Ballistae, Roman Onagers, English Trebuchets, and More Ancient Artillery*. Chicago: Chicago Review Press, 2004.

ON THE ROAD

U.S. Olympic Training Center
2800 Olympic Parkway
Chula Vista, CA 91915
619/482-6222

ON THE WEB

For more information on this topic, use FactHound.

1. Go to *www.facthound.com*
2. Type in this book ID: 0756533902
3. Click on the *Fetch It* button.

FactHound will find the best Web sites for you.

INDEX

ABOUT THE AUTHOR

Jana Voelke Studelska is a writer who lives in northern Minnesota, where there are many forests and lakes to explore.